X

The Kids' Career Library™

A Day in the Life of a
Park Ranger

Liza N. Burby

The Rosen Publishing Group's
PowerKids Press™
New York

Thanks to Eileen Fenton and Don Sommerfeld of the Fire Island National Park Service, U.S. Department of the Interior, for their help with this book.

Published in 1999 by The Rosen Publishing Group, Inc.
29 East 21st Street, New York, NY 10010

First Edition

Book Design: Erin McKenna

Photo Credits and Photo Illustrations: pp. 4, 7, 8, 11, 12, 15, 16, 20 by Christine Innamorato; p. 19 © 1996 PhotoDisc, Inc.

Burby, Liza N.
   A day in the life of a park ranger / by Liza N. Burby.
      p. cm. — (The kids' career library)
   Includes index.
   Summary: Describes the varied tasks and activities of a park ranger.
   ISBN 0-8239-5300-9
   1. Park rangers—Juvenile literature. 2. Park rangers—Vocational guidance—Juvenile literature. 3. Fenton, Eileen—Juvenile literature. [1. Park rangers. 2. Occupations.] I. Title. II. Series.
SB486.V62B87 1998
363.6'8'02373—DC21   98-7671
                                       CIP
                                       AC

Manufactured in the United States of America

Contents

People and Nature Together

Eileen Fenton works in a national park. As a park ranger, she helps protect animals, plants, and the land around them. She makes sure that people and nature get along. That is why she is trained to be a seasonal law **enforcer** (in-FOHR-sur). Eileen went to college, then she received special training to be a park ranger. That includes training to be an **emergency medical technician** (ih-MUR-jun-see MEH-duh-kul tek-NIH-shun), or EMT. She is also a trained firefighter.

◀ Being good with animals is very important for Eileen's job.

Ready for Anything

Eileen's job keeps her outdoors in all seasons and all weather. The park has a beach, and there are lots of animals, such as deer and horses. There are places to fish. And there are lots of visitors. Eileen has to be ready for anything. Her **uniform** (YOO-nuh-fohrm) includes a badge, a hat, and a bullet-proof vest. The vest helps keep Eileen safe during hunting season. She carries **binoculars** (buh-NAH-kyuh-lurz) and a camera. On her belt, Eileen wears a gun, a **baton** (buh-TAHN), handcuffs, a knife, a flashlight, and a radio.

Eileen is ready for work with all of her gear. ▶

In the Tower

Eileen starts her day at the ranger station. She has to climb many stairs to get all the way up to the **observation** (AHB-sur-VAY-shun) tower. The tower has windows on all four sides. This makes it easy for Eileen and the other rangers to see what is happening in the area they **patrol** (puh-TROHL). People come to the station all year to ask for information about interesting trails to **explore** (IK-splohr). Eileen shows them maps of the park and points them in the right direction. During hunting season, people come in to get **permits** (PUR-mits).

◀ Eileen keeps track of permits on her computer.

Patrolling the Beach

One of Eileen's jobs is to patrol the beach. She makes sure people follow park rules. If people catch too many fish or a kind they are not allowed to catch, she gives them a **ticket** (TIH-kut). People can also get a ticket if Eileen sees them feeding the deer. "Human food can make deer sick," she explains. "It also makes them come near cars. If deer aren't afraid of going near cars, they can get hit." Eileen wants people to care about park wildlife as much as she does.

Eileen tells people where it is safe to go on the beach. ▶

Many Ways to Get Around

Eileen has many different ways to get around the park. She walks a lot. Sometimes she drives a Jeep. It moves very slowly along the sandy beach. When she needs to get someplace very quickly, or if the beach is very crowded, she uses an **all-terrain vehicle** (AWL-tuh-RAYN VEE-ih-kul). This looks something like a motorcycle with four wheels. Other times Eileen may use a boat to patrol the shore. Eileen uses horses to get around when she is on wilderness patrol.

◀ All-terrain vehicles are good for places without smooth roads.

Ranger to the Rescue

Eileen often has to help **rescue** (RES-kyoo) people. She may have to help someone who is drowning or who has broken a leg. Eileen helps animals too. Many **injured** (IN-jurd) seals and whales wash up on her beach. Eileen takes pictures of them. She sends the photos to doctors and scientists who can help save the creatures. Sometimes Eileen rescues an animal simply by making sure no one else injures it. For example, when the piping plover bird lays its eggs in the sand, Eileen keeps trucks off the beach so that they won't crush the eggs.

Eileen uses her binoculars to watch ▶
for trouble all over the beach.

Camping and Teaching

Eileen is also in charge of the park's campgrounds. She makes sure they are clean and safe for campers. She also helps campers when they have questions about the park. Teaching visitors about the land and wildlife is another important part of Eileen's job. During camping season, she gives classes about the wildlife that live in her park so people can enjoy camping even more.

During the school year, students visit Eileen. Eileen teaches them about the things they will see around the park. She also tells students how she cares for the animals.

◄ Being a good teacher is part of being a good park ranger.

Learning About Wildlife

When Eileen is working, she often looks through her binoculars to watch the wildlife. She sees vultures, owls, ducks, geese, and foxes. She watches them to see how each animal **species** (SPEE-sheez) behaves. Today a deer family is watching Eileen closely. The mother deer wants to protect her baby. Eileen keeps her distance. She doesn't want to scare the deer.

Eileen says that the different animals sometimes make her laugh. Seagulls, for instance, often play by sliding down the sand dunes. That is fun for Eileen to watch.

Eileen always moves quietly around ▶ baby animals, like this baby deer.

A Piece of History

Park rangers don't just protect nature. Most national parks also have important buildings on the grounds. These are **historical** (hih-STOHR-ih-kul) buildings that have been **preserved** (pruh-ZURVD) so people can visit them. The building in Eileen's park is the William Floyd House. William Floyd was one of the people who signed the U.S. **Declaration of Independence** (deh-kluh-RAY-shun UV in-duh-PEN-dunts) in 1776. Today Eileen is checking to make sure the building is locked and safe. Another park ranger, Don Sommerfeld, takes care of this building.

◄ Eileen and the other rangers work as a team to care for the park.

Protecting the Land

Rangers have to make sure park visitors follow rules. The rules are to make sure that all visitors are careful in the park. "The park rangers' motto is To Protect the Land," Eileen says. She always wanted to work in **forestry** (FOHR-uh-stree). "I like working outdoors and with people. I also want to protect our **resources** (REE-sor-ses)," she says.

Eileen knows her work is an important part of preserving nature. She says that's "a good feeling." Before she leaves each day, Eileen takes a last look around the park and enjoys its beauty.

Glossary

all-terrain vehicle (AWL-tuh-RAYN VEE-ih-kul) A four-wheeled vehicle that looks like a motorcycle and can be driven on sand and dirt trails.

baton (buh-TAHN) A strong stick often carried by police officers.

binoculars (buh-NAH-kyuh-lurz) Hand-held lenses that make distant things appear closer.

Declaration of Independence (deh-kluh-RAY-shun UV in-duh-PEN-dunts) A paper signed on July 4, 1776, declaring that the American colonies were independent of Great Britain.

emergency medical technician (ih-MUR-jun-see MEH-duh-kul tek-NIH-shun) A person who takes care of sick people until they can get to a doctor.

enforcer (in-FOHR-sur) Someone who makes sure that laws are followed.

explore (IK-splohr) To examine something carefully.

forestry (FOHR-uh-stree) The science of planting and taking care of trees.

historical (hih-STOHR-ih-kul) When something is important in history.

injure (IN-jur) To harm or damage a person or thing.

observation (AHB-sur-VAY-shun) Looking at something carefully.

patrol (puh-TROHL) To protect a certain area by checking it often.

permit (PUR-mit) A written order giving permission to do something.

preserve (pruh-ZURV) To keep something safe from abuse and weather.

rescue (RES-kyoo) To save someone or something from danger or harm.

resource (REE-sors) A supply or source of energy or useful materials.

species (SPEE-sheez) A group of animals that are very much alike.

ticket (TIH-kut) A written order to appear in court if you've broken a law.

uniform (YOO-nuh-fohrm) Special clothes worn for a job.

Index